VOYAGER PROBES

Robots on an Interstellar Mission

Robyn Hardyman

PowerKiDS press™

NEW YORK

Published in 2017 by **The Rosen Publishing Group**
29 East 21st Street, New York, NY 10010

Copyright © 2017 by The Rosen Publishing Group

Produced for Rosen by Calcium

Editors for Calcium: Sarah Eason and Harriet McGregor
Designers for Calcium: Jennie Child
Picture researcher: Rachel Blount

Picture credits: Cover: Getty Images: CARLOS CLARIVAN/SCIENCE PHOTO LIBRARY (Voyager
image), Thinkstock: Pixtum (top banner), Shutterstock: Andrey_Kuzmin (metal plate), Thinkstock:
-strizh- (back cover illustration); Inside: NASA: Caltech/Palomar 24, JPL Caltech 10-11, 18, 20, 23,
27, 29; Shutterstock: Paulo Afonso 8, CHAINFOTO24 5, MarcelClemens 15, Naeblys 7; Wikimedia
Commons: NASA/JPL 17, NASA/MSFC 13.

CATALOGING-IN-PUBLICATION DATA
Names: Hardyman, Robyn.
Title: Voyager probes: robots on an interstellar mission / Robyn Hardyman.
Description: New York : Powerkids Press, 2017. | Series: Robots exploring space | Includes index.
Identifiers: ISBN 9781508151364 (pbk.) | ISBN 9781508151302 (library bound) |
    ISBN 9781508151197 (6 pack)
Subjects: LCSH: Voyager Project--Juvenile literature. | Space probes--Juvenile literature. |
    Outer space--Exploration--Juvenile literature.
Classification: LCC TL789.8.U6 H37 2017 | DDC 919.9'04--dc23

Manufactured in the United States of America
CPSIA Compliance Information: Batch #BS16PK. For Further Information contact Rosen Publishing, New York, New York at 1-800-237-9932

CONTENTS

The Mission

The *Voyager* mission is one of the greatest feats of exploration that humans have ever achieved. Since the launch in 1977 of the two robotic **probes** *Voyager 1* and *Voyager 2*, the mission has explored farther into space than any other before or since. In 2012, after traveling for 35 years, *Voyager 1* entered interstellar space for the very first time. This means that it reached beyond the edge of our solar system. *Voyager 2* is now well on its way to interstellar (between the stars) space, too.

At the beginning, the mission was more limited. The plan was that both *Voyager* probes would conduct closeup studies of the planets Jupiter and Saturn. They would look at Saturn's rings, and the larger moons of each planet.

Backup Plan

The reason for having two spacecraft was simple: it was a backup plan. The scientists wanted to investigate Saturn's moon, Titan. This was a key part of the mission. If *Voyager 1* failed to get a good look at Titan, *Voyager 2* would be able to change its flight path and take over.

Having two probes also allowed the mission to look at the largest four moons of Jupiter. Jupiter has very high levels of harmful **radiation**, one million times stronger than the radiation that surrounds Earth. This had caused problems with an earlier probe, *Pioneer 10*. So *Voyager 2* was kept farther away from Jupiter than *Voyager 1*, just in case the first probe was damaged. These robotic probes have been controlled from Earth for nearly 40 years, by people sending instructions to the **robots**' steering computers.

Our solar system
is one of billions
in our galaxy,
the Milky Way.

SPACE FIRST

THERE ARE SO MANY "FIRSTS" CONNECTED WITH THE
VOYAGER MISSION. IT HAS BEEN TRULY GROUNDBREAKING,
FROM THE WAY THE PROBES WERE BUILT AND CONTROLLED
TO THE DISCOVERIES THEY MADE. ALL THE MISSIONS THAT
HAVE FOLLOWED ON FROM VOYAGER HAVE BEEN PLANNED
AROUND INFORMATION LEARNED FROM THE MISSION.

The Groundwork

The *Voyager* mission is the work of the National Aeronautics and Space Administration (NASA), the U.S. government's agency for the national space program. Back in the 1970s, a huge team of scientists, engineers, and other experts worked to prepare and launch the two *Voyager* robotic probes.

Built to Last?

Voyager 1 and *Voyager 2* were not really designed for the amazing mission they are on today. When the project began, they were built to last for just 5 years. NASA thought that would be long enough to get them to Jupiter and Saturn. They were designed to travel for 10 astronomical units (AUs). These are the units scientists use to measure the vast distances in space. One AU is 10 times the distance from Earth to the sun. So *Voyager* was built to travel 100 times farther than from Earth to the sun!

The *Voyager* mission was set up to take advantage of a rare opportunity. Every 175 years or so, the **orbits** of the outer planets of the solar system, Jupiter, Saturn, Uranus, and Neptune, place them

SPACE FIRST

VOYAGER IS THE LONGEST-RUNNING SPACE EXPLORATION MISSION EVER. BY 2015, IT HAD BEEN IN OPERATION FOR 38 YEARS.

Voyager reached
Jupiter in 1979.

in a particular arrangement. Their locations mean that a spacecraft can swing from one planet to another without needing to have a powerful onboard **propulsion system**. As a spacecraft flies past each planet, the force of the planet's gravity pulls at the spacecraft and bends its flightpath. This action speeds up the spacecraft enough to send it on to the next planet. As a result of this, the flight time to Neptune was reduced from 30 years to 12 years.

It was important to plan carefully the **trajectories** that the probes would take. They had to reach their destinations at the best times, and in the best positions, to study the planets closely, and then move on. Scientists looked at more than 10,000 possible trajectories. Finally, they selected the two that they thought were the best. The trajectories would allow both probes to study Jupiter and its moon Io, and Saturn and its moon Titan. The path for *Voyager 2* would also give it the option to fly on to Uranus and Neptune.

All About Voyager

The *Voyager* probes were built almost 40 years ago. Our knowledge of computers and of technology in general was much less advanced then than it is today. This is one of the things that makes this robotic mission so extraordinary. These relatively simple machines have traveled billions of miles, at around 37,000 miles (59,550 km) per hour, for several decades, and they are still going. They are still scientifically useful, too, because they continue to send back **data** to teach us more about space.

The two probes are exactly the same. They were built at NASA's Jet Propulsion Laboratory in Pasadena, California.

Huge antennae receive data sent from the *Voyager* probes to Earth.

Each probe is made of 65,000 parts. They have instruments to conduct 10 different investigations. These include cameras to take photos, **sensors** to detect many different kinds of **particles**, and radios. The onboard computers are tiny. A smartphone today has about 250,000 times more memory than *Voyager*'s computer.

Power

The probes are powered by plutonium batteries. Plutonium is a radioactive substance that creates heat, which is converted into electricity. Plutonium does not produce a lot of power, but it can produce it for a very long time, perfect for unmanned space missions.

The *Voyager* probes are controlled by telerobotics. This means they are controlled remotely, or from a distance. This is done using NASA's powerful Deep Space Network (DSN), a group of large antennae and other communication facilities in the United States, Spain, and Australia. These sites are equally spaced around Earth, so at any time one of them can track the location of the probes as Earth rotates. Together they send instructions to the probes, and receive information back from them. NASA knows exactly where the probes are at any one time.

The Golden Records

Sending probes out into our solar system raises the exciting question of whether some other intelligent form of life may find them one day. The team behind the *Voyager* mission wanted to address this question. They put on board each probe a collection of messages from Earth.

The messages are recorded on two golden **LP records**. These are 12-inch (30-cm) gold-plated copper disks. On them are stored sounds and images to show the richness and variety of life on our planet. There are 115 photos of people and places from around the world. There are sounds from nature, such as surf and whales, and sounds that people have created, such as music from different eras in history and different cultures. There are also spoken messages in 55 languages from throughout human history, including Akkadian, a language spoken 6,000 years ago in the Middle East, and

The cover of the golden record explains how to play it to unlock its contents.

many languages of today. The English message is, "Hello from the children of planet Earth." The message in Mandarin is, "Hope everyone is well. We are thinking about you all. Please come here to visit when you have time." The cover of each record explains with diagrams how to play it and unlock the messages it contains.

Making a Selection

It was a difficult job to choose what to put on these records to sum up life on Earth. A committee was created to make the selection. It was led by Dr. Carl Sagan of Cornell University. At the time he said, "The spacecraft will be encountered and the record played only if there are advanced spacefaring civilizations in interstellar space. But the launching of this bottle into the cosmic ocean says something very hopeful about life on this planet."

SPACE FIRST

IT WAS DR. CARL SAGAN'S IDEA TO FIX THE GOLDEN RECORDS TO THE VOYAGER PROBES. SAGAN'S YOUNG SON, NICK, RECORDED THE ENGLISH MESSAGE ON THEM. ALTHOUGH IT IS UNLIKELY ANYONE WILL EVER FIND AND UNLOCK THEM, THEIR PRESENCE ON VOYAGER CONNECTS US ON EARTH POWERFULLY TO THE PROBES AS THEY DRIFT THROUGH OUTER SPACE.

Launch

After many years of planning, the time came to launch. All spacecraft must be propelled (pushed upward) into space with great speed and power to send them out beyond Earth's **atmosphere**. The only way to achieve this speed and power is with a rocket. For the *Voyager* mission, the rocket chosen was a Titan III-E Centaur rocket. Titan rockets burned liquid **hydrogen** and liquid oxygen to create a massive amount of power.

Different Flight paths

On August 20, 1977, the first probe was launched from the NASA Kennedy Space Center at Cape Canaveral, Florida. On September 5, the second probe was launched. The two probes had different flight paths, and were traveling at different speeds. The first probe to be launched was called *Voyager 2*, and the second probe launched was called *Voyager 1*. This was because the flightpath of the second probe was more direct and it was traveling faster, so it would reach Jupiter first.

Rocket Performance

In the first launch, the rocket worked perfectly. In the second launch, the rocket burned out too early, and there was a danger it would run out of power. It turned out that the rocket ended its mission with less than 4 seconds of burning time remaining! Once up in space, the probes could control their movement and keep steady as they sped forward. Each probe was built with six pairs of **thrusters**, to control its rolling and pitching. Three pairs were the primary thrusters, and three pairs were for backup.

SPACE DISCOVERY

AFTER THE LAUNCH OF VOYAGER, NASA BEGAN TO DEVELOP NEW SPACECRAFT THAT NEEDED A DIFFERENT KIND OF ROCKET FOR THEIR LAUNCHING, SUCH AS THE SPACE SHUTTLE. THESE ROCKETS HAD THE ADVANTAGE OF BEING REUSABLE.

Blast off! *Voyager 2* is successfully launched.

Jupiter and Saturn

Voyager 1 reached Jupiter in 1979, and Saturn in 1980. *Voyager 2* was close behind, visiting Jupiter in 1979, and Saturn in 1981. At both planets, these robotic probes made more discoveries than the scientists had even dreamed possible.

Gas Planets

The *Voyager* probes taught us that Jupiter and Saturn have no solid surface; each is made of a massive atmosphere of gases. Between them, the probes took 33,000 photos of Jupiter and its moons. They revealed for the first time that Jupiter has rings, and that its atmosphere is permanently stormy! One of Jupiter's moons, Europa, has an icy crust. *Voyager* revealed that there seems to be a salty ocean locked beneath this crust. Could this ocean be a place where living things exist? Scientists are still exploring this very exciting idea.

SPACE DISCOVERY

ONE OF THE GREATEST SURPRISES WAS THE DISCOVERY THAT THERE ARE VOLCANOES ON JUPITER'S MOON IO. THIS WAS THE FIRST TIME VOLCANOES HAD BEEN SEEN BEYOND EARTH, AND ON IO THEY ARE 10 TIMES MORE ACTIVE. **ERUPTIONS** FROM THESE VOLCANOES SEND SULFUR AND OTHER SUBSTANCES OUT INTO JUPITER'S **MAGNETIC FIELD.**

At Saturn's equator the winds blow from east to west, but farther to the north and south they blow in both directions.

At Saturn, the discoveries were just as amazing. Saturn's icy rings were well-known, but for the first time *Voyager* revealed details of what they are made of, and that they are pulled out of shape by Saturn's moons nearby. *Voyager* explored Saturn's gases and found they are mostly hydrogen and **helium**. The probes also discovered that the winds around Saturn's equator (line around the middle of the planet) blow at an incredible 1,100 miles (1,770 km) per hour.

Another amazing detail that *Voyager* was able to send back is that one day on Saturn lasts for 10 hours, 39 minutes, and 24 seconds of Earth time. This is how long it takes for Saturn to rotate once. This fast rotation makes the north and south poles of the planet flattened. This is possible because the planet is made of gases and is not solid.

Uranus and Neptune

After *Voyager 2*'s mission to Saturn, the scientists realized that this extraordinary robotic probe could keep going. It could reach Uranus, and it later became clear that *Voyager 2* could even reach Neptune, the farthest planet from the sun. *Voyager 2* did reach these planets: Uranus in 1986 and Neptune in 1989.

Magnetism, Storms, Rings, and Moons

No one had known that Uranus has its own magnetic field, until it was identified by *Voyager*. Uranus also has rings, and *Voyager* found that they may consist of pieces of an old moon that was smashed up in a collision long ago. It also measured the length of a day on Uranus, and found it is 17 hours and 14 minutes. Finally, *Voyager* found 11 new moons around Uranus, and visited 16 altogether.

In August 1989, *Voyager 2* was the first spacecraft to observe Neptune. No other spacecraft has visited the planet since. The probe passed about 3,000 miles (4,950 km) above this gas giant's north pole. It discovered huge storms swirling around, including a massive Great Dark Spot that is about the size of Earth. The winds in these storms are the fastest in the solar system, at 1,200 miles (2,000 km) per hour. It also revealed that Neptune has four rings around it, showing that all four of the giant planets have rings.

Voyager also passed about 25,000 miles (40,000 km) from Neptune's largest moon, Triton. It saw huge geysers, or vents, erupting, spewing nitrogen gas and dust particles several miles high.

SPACE DISCOVERY

ONE OF THE MOST AMAZING THINGS
VOYAGER SHOWED US WAS FIVE NEW
MOONS AROUND NEPTUNE, BRINGING
ITS TOTAL NUMBER OF MOONS TO
EIGHT. THEY WERE NAMED AFTER
ANCIENT GREEK WATER GODDESSES:
NAIAD, THALASSA, DESPINA,
PROTEUS, AND GALATEA.

Voyager 2 took
this picture of
Neptune from a
distance of
4.4 million miles
(7.1 million km).

The planets of our solar system had been seen as never before. On February 14, 1990, *Voyager 1* took the last photos of the original mission. From beyond Neptune, about 3.7 billion miles (6 billion km) from Earth, *Voyager 1* turned its camera back toward our solar system and took a series of final photos. It captured Neptune, Uranus, Saturn, Jupiter, Venus, and Earth.

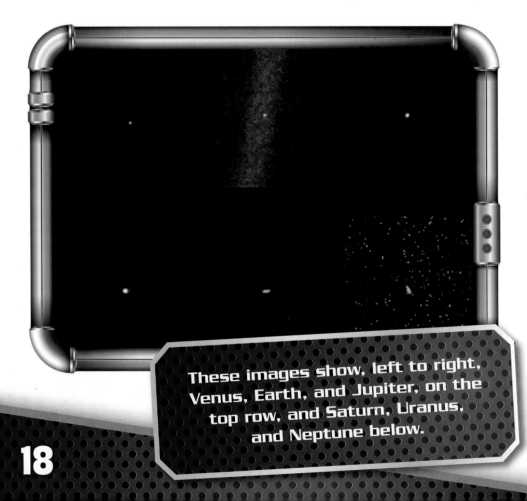

These images show, left to right, Venus, Earth, and Jupiter, on the top row, and Saturn, Uranus, and Neptune below.

After this, *Voyager 1*'s cameras were switched off forever. There would be little for them to see in the vast, dark emptiness of space. The controllers needed to save as much onboard power as possible for the next exciting stage of the mission: *Voyager* was going interstellar! The Voyager Interstellar Mission (ISM) would first explore the outermost edges of our solar system, and then leave it, to travel through the space between the stars in our galaxy, the Milky Way. This truly was a new frontier.

Influence of the Sun

Voyager 1 was looking for the edge of the **solar wind**. This wind flows outward from the sun at 1 million miles (1.6 million km) per hour. The solar wind forms a "bubble" around the solar system that is called the **heliosphere**. The edge of the heliosphere is called the **heliopause**. Beyond the heliopause is the interstellar wind.

Could *Voyager 1* and *2* travel beyond the influence of the sun? How far was it to the heliopause? How long would it take? The team estimated that it was 50–150 AU. Out at Neptune, *Voyager 1* had traveled 30 AUs, so it had a long way to go. It was not certain that its plutonium battery would have enough power to work the instruments needed to record the journey and relay the information. The battery was losing power every year. How long could it last?

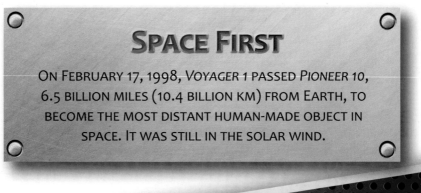

SPACE FIRST

On February 17, 1998, *Voyager 1* passed *Pioneer 10*, 6.5 billion miles (10.4 billion km) from Earth, to become the most distant human-made object in space. It was still in the solar wind.

Success!

As *Voyager 1* and *2* traveled through the heliosphere, they collected groundbreaking data about the strength and direction of the solar wind. There is a point within the heliosphere where the solar wind slows suddenly. It slows because it is hit by gases coming the other way, from beyond the heliopause, out between the stars. This point is called the **termination shock**. Scientists knew it existed, but its exact location was one of the great unanswered questions in space science.

Voyager 1 crossed the termination shock and headed for the edge of the solar system.

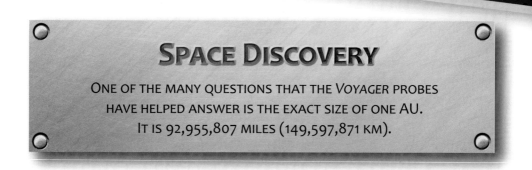

In December 2004, the instruments on *Voyager 1* recorded that it has crossed the termination shock. It was about 8.7 billion miles (14 billion km) from the sun. The speed of the solar wind dropped to about 400,000 miles (640,000 km) per hour.

Edge of the Heliosphere

In August 2007, *Voyager 2* also crossed the termination shock. Both probes were now operating in the outer reaches of the heliosphere. There they were still under the influence of the sun's magnetic field and particles in the solar wind. As they traveled farther, data from the probes' instruments showed that the solar wind was slowing even more. The solar wind produces low-energy particles. Gradually the number of these particles detected by *Voyager 1* declined. By 2010, the instruments on *Voyager 1* were detecting more of the kind of particles present in interstellar space, beyond the heliosphere. These are high-energy particles.

The scientists at NASA were incredibly excited. Already their *Voyager* mission had provided enough new information to rewrite the textbooks on astronomy. This was more than they could have hoped for, back in 1977. Now they were on the brink of another breakthrough. This robot probe was about to leave our solar system and venture out into the space between the stars in the Milky Way.

No Final Frontier

Finally, on August 25, 2012, one of the most exciting things ever seen in space exploration happened. *Voyager 1* crossed the heliopause and left the heliosphere. It was now traveling in interstellar space! It was incredibly difficult to interpret the data from *Voyager 1* that showed this, so NASA did not announce that it had happened until 2013.

Measurements in Interstellar Space

Voyager 1's crossover into interstellar space allowed the scientists to figure out an accurate distance from the sun to the heliopause. They estimated that the heliopause is nearly 125 AUs from the sun, nearly 125 times farther than the distance between the sun and Earth. Our powerful sun extends its influence across this incredible distance, with its solar wind. This blows past our planet and all the other planets. The farthest planet, Neptune, is 30 AUs from the sun, so the wind blows for another 95 AUs before it ends.

Voyager 2 has been speeding through the heliosphere since it left Neptune in 1989. The NASA team expects it to enter interstellar space during 2016 or 2017. They are very excited about this event, particularly because *Voyager 2* has on board an instrument that can make important measurements. The same instrument on *Voyager 1* stopped working before it entered interstellar space. *Voyager 2* will be able to measure the temperature and other details about the space it is flying through.

Voyager 1 has left the heliosphere and *Voyager 2* is not too far behind.

Where Are They Now?

    Voyager 1 is traveling through interstellar space at about 37,800 miles (61,000 km) per hour. At the end of 2015, it was 12.4 billion miles (20 billion km) from the sun. The experts think that it is still being very slightly influenced by the solar wind, even though it has left the heliosphere. They expect that this will continue for another 10 years. By 2025, they think *Voyager 1* will have reached "pristine" interstellar space, where there is no effect at all from the sun's solar wind.

Voyager 1 is now traveling through interstellar space.

At the end of 2015, *Voyager 2* was still in the heliosphere, about 10.2 billion miles (16.4 billion km) from the sun. Both probes are using their backup thrusters to control their turning and rolling.

Signals from Space

We know where these amazing probes are because they are both still sending data back to Earth, all day every day. The instruments on board still have enough battery power to continue working, though this power is decreasing all the time. The information they send back about their surroundings is still being received through the powerful antennae of NASA's DSN. It takes a lengthy period of time to communicate with these distant robots, so the scientists must plan ahead. A signal sent from Earth travels at the speed of light, but even at that speed it takes more than 17 hours to reach the *Voyager* probes. The signals coming back take the same length of time to reach Earth. Once they are received, they are sent to teams around the United States to be analyzed.

SPACE DISCOVERY

THE TRANSMITTERS ON BOARD THE *VOYAGER* PROBES THAT SEND THE DATA SIGNALS TO EARTH ARE EXTREMELY LOW POWERED. THE SIGNALS THEY SEND HAVE JUST 20 WATTS, WHICH IS THE SAME AS THE POWER OF A DIM LIGHT BULB. BY THE TIME THESE SIGNALS REACH EARTH, THEY ARE JUST ONE BILLIONTH OF A BILLIONTH OF A WATT, YET THEY CAN STILL BE DETECTED. THIS MEANS THAT THE ROBOTS CAN SEND INFORMATION ABOUT WHAT IS HAPPENING IN SPACE ACROSS HUGE DISTANCES, BACK TO EARTH.

Keeping Going

The team of people who have worked on the *Voyager* mission, since 1977, is enormous. Many scientists who began their careers as juniors on the team are still involved with it today, as senior members. They feel great affection for *Voyager 1* and *2*, after so many years. Professor Ed Stone has been the Voyager Project Scientist since 1972. He is still in that role today. As he says, "We all knew we were on a mission of discovery. We just had no idea how much discovery there would be. We just kept finding things we didn't know were there to be found."

Learning About Space

Many people are still involved in keeping in touch with the *Voyager* probes, maintaining these robots that are billions of miles away. Most of the instruments have now been switched off, but the ones that are operational need to be watched by a team of controllers. One of them described his job: "I just love to think of everything, all those 65,000 parts on each craft, working up there," he says. "Oh man, it really is something. Every time we come in here, it is just a gift. And you know that one day it could stop." It is important that these spacecraft, that have achieved so much, can be kept going for as long as possible. It will be a long time before we have any other spacecraft out in interstellar space, so this is a valuable opportunity to learn as much as we can for as long as we can.

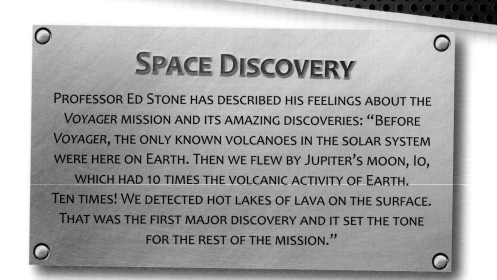

SPACE DISCOVERY

PROFESSOR ED STONE HAS DESCRIBED HIS FEELINGS ABOUT THE VOYAGER MISSION AND ITS AMAZING DISCOVERIES: "BEFORE VOYAGER, THE ONLY KNOWN VOLCANOES IN THE SOLAR SYSTEM WERE HERE ON EARTH. THEN WE FLEW BY JUPITER'S MOON, IO, WHICH HAD 10 TIMES THE VOLCANIC ACTIVITY OF EARTH. TEN TIMES! WE DETECTED HOT LAKES OF LAVA ON THE SURFACE. THAT WAS THE FIRST MAJOR DISCOVERY AND IT SET THE TONE FOR THE REST OF THE MISSION."

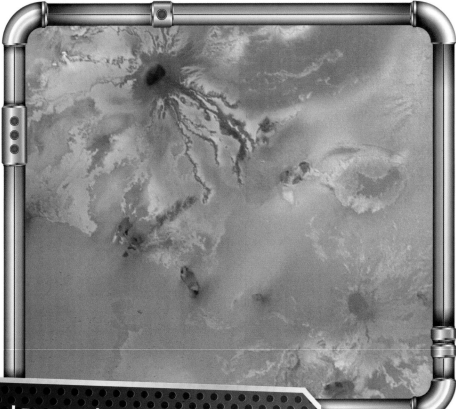

Lava can be seen flowing from the volcanoes on Io.

Mission Complete?

The robotic *Voyager* mission has achieved all it set out to do, and so much more. It has answered important questions about the planets and the solar system, and raised many new ones about the world of interstellar space. The instruments are still sending data, and should continue to do so until about 2020. By that time, *Voyager 1* will be 13.8 billion miles (22.1 billion km) from the sun, and *Voyager 2* will be 11.4 billion miles (18.4 billion km) from the sun.

What Next?

The engineers will switch off the instruments one by one, to conserve battery power. In about 2025, the last instrument will turn off. The two probes will continue to send what are called engineering signals, for another 5–7 years. Scientists are thinking about what experiments could be done with these signals, before the probes finally fall completely silent.

These extraordinary probes will continue to drift through space. Eventually they will pass other stars in the Milky Way galaxy. In about 40,000 years, *Voyager 1* will travel to within 9.3 trillion miles (14.9 trillion km) of another **planetary system** in a constellation (group) of stars called Camelopardalis. In about 296,000 years, *Voyager 2* will pass 25 trillion miles (40 trillion km) from Sirius, the brightest star in the sky. These times and distances are hard for us to imagine, but for *Voyager 1* and *Voyager 2* there may be nothing to prevent them wandering the Milky Way forever.

Voyager 2 took this photo of Jupiter's moon, Europa. Its outer ice crust is thought to be 62 miles (100 km) thick.

SPACE DISCOVERY

COULD ANOTHER LIFE FORM OUT THERE DISCOVER VOYAGER IN THE FUTURE? COULD IT UNLOCK THE MESSAGES WE LEFT IN THE GOLDEN RECORDS, AND LEARN ABOUT A DISTANT LIFE IN OUR SOLAR SYSTEM FROM LONG, LONG AGO? IF THERE ARE OTHER LIFE FORMS IN SPACE, PERHAPS THE VOYAGER PROBES WILL TEACH THEM ABOUT HUMANS AND OUR LIFE ON EARTH!

GLOSSARY

antennae Devices that send and receive radio signals.

atmosphere A layer of gases that surround a planet or moon.

data Information.

eruptions Processes in which volcanoes spew out substances from beneath their surfaces.

galaxy A vast group of stars.

heliopause The edge of the heliosphere.

heliosphere The area of space in our solar system influenced by the sun's solar wind.

helium A substance that is usually a gas on Earth.

hydrogen A substance that is usually a gas on Earth, but can exist as a liquid if the temperature is cold enough.

LP records Long-playing records, disks with grooves that store data such as music and images.

magnetic field A region around an object where the force of magnetism exists.

orbits Travels around an object in a circular way.

particles Tiny pieces of matter.

planetary system A set of planets in orbit around a star.

probes Robots that are programmed to explore a particular area of space.

propulsion system A system that gives a driving force to push an object in a certain direction.

radiation Energy or particles sent out by a substance.

robots Machines that are programmed to carry out particular jobs.

sensors Devices that react to particular aspects of the environment, such as light waves.

solar wind The flow of charged particles from the sun.

termination shock The place in the heliosphere where the solar wind meets the interstellar wind.

thrusters Small engines that are used to change the direction or speed of a spacecraft.

trajectories Routes taken by moving objects.

FOR MORE INFORMATION

Books

Aguilar, David A. *Space Encyclopedia*. Washington, D.C.: National Geographic Kids, 2013.

Knowledge Encyclopedia: Space! New York, NY: DK Children, 2015.

Sagan, Carl. *Cosmos*. New York, NY: Ballantine Books, 2013.

Stott, Carole. *Space Exploration* (DK Eyewitness). New York, NY: DK Children, 2014.

Websites

Due to the changing nature of Internet links, PowerKids Press has developed an online list of websites related to the subject of this book. This site is updated regularly. Please use this link to access the list: **www.powerkidslinks.com/res/voyager**

INDEX